FOR A BASKETBALL FAN WHO HAS EVERYTHING

A Funny Basketball Book

Team Golfwell and Bruce Miller

FOR A BASKETBALL FAN WHO HAS EVERYTHING: A Funny Basketball Book, Copyright © 2023, Pacific Trust Holdings NZ Ltd. All rights are reserved for the collective work only. No part of this book may be reproduced or transmitted in any form or by any means, electronic or mechanical, including photocopying, recording, or by any information storage and retrieval system, without written permission from the author, except for brief quotations as would be used in a review.

This is the eighteenth book in the series, *For People Who Have Everything*. Cover by Queen Graphics. All images are from Creative Commons or Shutterstock.

ISBN 978-1-99-104836-3 (Ingram Spark B&W paperback)

ISBN 978-1-99-104837-0 (Ingram Spark B&W hardback)

ISBN 978-1-99-104838-7 (Ingram Spark Color paperback)

ISBN 978-1-99-104839-4 (Ingram Spark Color hardback)

ISBN 9798851687372 (KDP B&W paperback)

ISBN 9798851689338 (KDP B&W hardcover)

ISBN 9798851690525 (KDP Color paperback)

ISBN 9798851691508 (KDP Color hardback)

For a Basketball Fan Who Has Everything: A Funny Basketball Book

Dedication

To every basketball player, from youngsters to seniors, no matter where you are, have been, or want to be in your game.

And to all professional basketball players, owners, managers, coaches, announcers, personalities, and everyone who gave us so many unforgettable moments in this magical sport! Thank you very much for it all and for moments to come!

For a Basketball Fan Who Has Everything: A Funny Basketball Book

"If I weren't earning $3 million a year to dunk a basketball, most people on the street would run in the other direction if they saw me coming."

—Charles Barkley

Charles Barkley

For a Basketball Fan Who Has Everything: A Funny Basketball Book

What you need. "Doesn't matter where you come from, what you have or don't have... All you need are faith in God, an undying passion for what you do and what you choose to do in this life, and a relentless drive and the will to do whatever it takes to be successful in whatever you put your mind to."

-- **Stephen Curry**

Being tall. "They always asked me if I played basketball because I was tall. They stopped asking me that when I asked them if they played mini golf."

-- Anon.

Who invented basketball and the rules? James Naismith invented basketball in 1891 when he was asked by his boss at a YMCA to invent an indoor winter activity in Springfield, Massachusetts. He was a Canadian American of Scottish descent, and a Physical Education teacher, physician, Christian chaplain, and sports coach. [1]

After he moved to the US from Canada, he wrote the original basketball rule book and founded the University of Kansas basketball program.

James Naismith

Makes you wonder. "The only mystery in life is why kamikaze pilots wore helmets."

-- **Al McGuire**, college basketball coach, and broadcaster, the head coach at Marquette University from 1964 to 1977. He won a national championship in his final season at Marquette and was inducted into the Naismith Memorial Basketball Hall of Fame in 1992.

Nervous? "Nervous means you want to play. Scared means you don't want to play."

— **Sherman Alexie**, excerpt from "The Absolutely True Diary of a Part-Time Indian"

Fastest fouling out. On December 29, 1997, in a game against the Chicago Bulls, Bubba Wells set the record for the shortest amount of playing time before fouling out in an NBA regular season game. [2]

This is how that happened. In the third quarter of the game, Mavericks coach Don Nelson used a tactic later known as "Hack-a-Shaq" by having Bubba purposely foul Dennis Rodman *(who had a lifetime 58.4% free throw shooting average)* six (6) times in a total of two minutes and 43 seconds. That's a record for the shortest time anyone has ever fouled out in a game and probably will not ever be broken.

Even though Rodman had a bad free throw percentage, it backfired in this game when he made 9 out of the 12 free throws and the Chicago Bulls won 111-105.

Dennis Rodman

Don't have to like it all the time. "There's a great quote by Julius Irving that went, 'Being a professional is doing the things you love to do, on the days you don't feel like doing them.'"

— **David Halberstam**, an excerpt from "Everything They Had: Sports Writing."

The Mathematician, Physicist, and Engineer. A mathematician, a physicist, and an engineer are asked to measure the volume of a basketball.

The mathematician grabs a cord to measure its circumference and from there works out its volume.

The physicist pushes the basketball into a bucket of water and measures the water displacement.

The engineer looks it up on the catalog.

March Madness little known fact. In the year 2008, the four number-one seeds won their regionals. In the long history of March Madness, 2008 was the only year ever that the four number one seeds won their regional finals and progressed to the final four.

The teams were UCLA, Kansas, Memphis, and North Carolina and Kansas won the NCAA Championship.

Kids are great, but... "That's one of the best things about our business, all the kids you get to meet.

"It's a shame they have to go on and grow up to be regular people and come to the games and call you names."

For a Basketball Fan Who Has Everything: A Funny Basketball Book

-- Charles Barkley

Basketball Rule Question 1. John's team is leading 89 to 88 with 7 seconds left in the game and he's been playing hard the whole game. Now he's dehydrated and has a low blood sugar level leaving him disorientated. He takes a pass from a teammate in the backcourt and being confused and he shoots the ball from the floor inside the three-point line through his own basket and gets nothing but net. Then the buzzer sounds at the end of the game. Does John's team lose 90-89?

A. John's team loses since his basket counts for the other team.

B. John gets a free throw at his own basket.

C. John tells the referee it shouldn't be a basket for the other team since he was distracted by a beautiful girl in the stands who pointed at the wrong basket.

D. The referee says, "That's illegal!" and rules it doesn't count for anything and John's team wins!

Answers begin on page 97.

No limits.

"Never let anyone lower your goals.

Others' expectations of you are determined by their limitations of life.

The sky is your limit, son.

Always shoot for the sun and you will shine."

— **Kwame Alexander**, The Crossover

Amazing last 20 seconds! In Maine in February 2023, two high school teams played to an incredible finish. It was a contest between the Thornton Academy Trojans and the Bonny Eagle Scots, and with 20.9 seconds left in the game, the score was 47 to 45 in favor of Thornton.

However, a 3-pointer gave the Scots a 48-47 lead just a few seconds later. The Trojans shortly regained the lead and were up 50-48 with only 8.8 seconds remaining.

The Scots then scored and with an added free throw and regained the lead with only 1.3 seconds left making it a 51-50 game.

Fasten your seatbelts. The wild finish only got more dramatic. Now it looked very promising for the Bonny Eagles but Thornton had 1.3 seconds left. That's 1.3 seconds!

Thornton inbounded with a very long inbound pass that was caught 30 feet away from the basket. Taking one dribble, the shot was released at the top of the key just after the red-light end of the game flashed signaling the end of the 4th quarter.

Since the shot was made after the red-light went off, it was clear to everyone in the arena the shot should not have counted. But a video broadcast of the game showed the game clock having 0.2 seconds left!

Controversy arose about whether time had run out or not. The referee said the shot counted and Thornton won 52-51.

Thornton Academy subsequently won the state championship over the weekend, defeating South Portland, 82-61.

Mistakes. "It's OK to make mistakes. That's how we learn. When we compete, we make mistakes."

— **Kareem Abdul-Jabbar**

Most points scored by halftime. In the 1990-91 season, the Suns scored 107 points from 50 and 57-point quarters in the first half against Golden State. This set the current record.

The Suns didn't stop in the second half and scored a total of 173 points in the game.

The amazing thing about the first half was the Suns scored 107 points in the 24-minute first half without making a 3–pointer. [3]

Anything is possible. "My whole life, people have doubted me. My mom did. People told me in high school I was too short and not fast enough to play basketball. They didn't know my story. Because if they did, they'd know that anything is possible."

— **Jimmy Butler**. NBA player for the Miami Heat Nicknamed "Jimmy Buckets" and "Playoff Jimmy." He is a six-time NBA All-Star, a five-time All-NBA Team honoree, and an Olympic gold medalist (2016 Summer Olympics).

More than serious. "I am more than just a serious basketball fan. I am a life-long addict. I was addicted from birth, in fact, because I was born in Kentucky."

— **Hunter S. Thompson.** Journalist and author.

Individual record for most points. The most points scored in an NBA game was 100 by none other than 7' 1" Wilt "The Stilt" Chamberlain. It was a game that happened in March 1962 while playing for the Philadelphia Warriors. The Warriors won that game with a total of 162 team points.

Wilt shot 36-for-63 from the floor and 28-for-32 from the free throw line.

Wilt averaged 50.2 points per game for the Warriors that season. The closest anyone has ever come to breaking that record was the late, great Kobe Bryant. He scored 81 against the Raptors in 2006.

Wilt Chamberlain

Must pay attention. "Fans never fall asleep at our games, because they're afraid they might get hit by a pass."

    -- **George Raveling.** College player and coach.

Hard to get tickets. The attendance record for a single game is 62,046, which was a game between the Chicago Bulls and the Hawks in 1998. Jordan was retiring and the Hawks chose to play at the Dome, which is Atlanta's biggest sports facility.

The huge crowd saw Mike score 34 points in an 89-74 win over the Hawks.

This record was set in the regular season.

Another record involves a game played in Texas. Everything is big in Texas, as we all know. The 2010 NBA All-Star Game played in Arlington, holds the all-time NBA attendance record with 108,713.

Selfish and Unselfish. "To be successful you must be selfish, or else you never achieve. And once you get to your highest level, then you must be unselfish. Stay reachable. Stay in touch. Don't isolate."

— **Michael Jordan**

Critics in the seats sayings.

- "I've seen more bricks here than at a construction site."
- "Pack your suitcase because that's traveling."
- "There's always a need for bricklayers."
- "You must be from Sweden because you got no Finnish."
- "A million-dollar move with a $2 shot."
- "I hope you taped your ankles."
- "Your loss is my game."

What a win is like. "Winning is like deodorant – it comes up, and a lot of things don't stink."

-- **Doc Rivers**. NBA player and coach.

Coming alive. "We learn to make a shell for ourselves when we are young and then spend the rest of our lives hoping for someone to reach inside and touch us. Just touch us—anything more than that would be too much for us to bear."

— **Bill Russell**. Five-time NBA Most Valuable Player and a 12-time NBA All-Star. He was the centerpiece of the Celtics dynasty that won 11 NBA championships during his 13-year career.

Humble beginnings. Nikola Jokić was born in the city of Sobor in the northern part of Serbia. [4] He grew up in a cramped two-bedroom apartment that housed him and his two brothers, both parents and his grandmother. His father was an agricultural engineer. [5]

Nikola developed a love of basketball early in his life playing with his two older brothers, Strahinja and Nemanja, who were a decade older.

"The Joker" now is a five-time NBA All-Star and he's been named to the All-NBA Team on five occasions (including three first-team selections), and won the NBA Most Valuable Player

Award for the 2020–21 and 2021–22 seasons and the MVP for the NBA finals 2023 by leading the Nuggets over Miami in 5 games.

One of the remarks the media often observes about "The Joker" is that he's a thinker. He's always thinking, and many say he plays basketball from the neck up. That seems to be working well for him!

He started as a chubby teenager and told reporters, "Don't bet against the fat boy."

Nikola Jokic

Just ask me. "Ask me to steal, block out, sacrifice, lead, dominate, anything. But it's not what you ask of me -- it's what I ask of myself."

— **LeBron James**

Making sure you win. The biggest margin of victory in an NBA game involved a game in the 1991-92 season when the Cleveland Cavaliers beat the Miami Heat 148-80 just a week after the Heat beat the Cavs in Miami.

The Cavs only had a "slim lead" of 20 at halftime but poured it on in the second half scoring 75 points to the Heat's 27.

You don't need your five best players. "Some say you have to use your five best players, but I found out you win with the five that fit together best as a team."

— **Red Auerbach**. Mr. Auerbach set NBA records with 938 wins and nine championships. That was a record until Phil Jackson coached 11 championship teams (Bulls and the Lakers).

After Red's coaching retirement in 1966, he served as president and front-office executive of the Celtics until his death. As general manager and team president of the Celtics, he won an additional seven NBA titles for a grand total of 16 over 29 years, the most of any individual in NBA history, making him one of the most successful team executives in the history of North American professional sports.

Red Auerbach

Longest win streak. When you put Wilt Chamberlain, Elgin Baylor, and Jerry West together on one team amazing things happen. To this day, the 33-game winning streak still stands while they were on their way to the NBA championship. [6]

Not a high scorer? If you really want to be a high scorer, take up golf.

Don't have to be perfect. "No one plays this or any game perfectly. It's the guy who recovers from his mistakes who wins."

— **Phil Jackson**, former head coach of the Chicago Bulls from 1989 to 1998, leading them to six NBA championships. He then coached the Los Angeles Lakers from 1999 to 2004 and again from 2005 to 2011; the team won five league titles under his leadership. Phil's 11 NBA titles as a coach surpassed the previous record of nine set by Red Auerbach.

Don't intentionally foul this guy. What's the record for the highest free throw percentage? Jose Calderon missed just three out of 151 free throw attempts for the entire 2008-09 season. That's 98%! He broke a 28-year record previously set by Calvin Murphy (95.8 percent).

Jose didn't miss a free throw until late January, then he missed two of his next six attempts but that was it.

Overall, Jose shot 90 percent or better from the free throw line over his 16-year career.

Over 50-point games. Michael Jordan had 31 games where he scored more than 50 points. That seems amazing but going back in time, the record for most 50-point games is held by Wilt Chamberlain who had 118 fifty-point games.

What might be even more amazing was the fact that in 32 of those 118 games, Wilt scored more than 60 points.

It ain't easy. "I try to make it look easy, but the behind-the-scenes stuff is the challenge."

-- **Stephen Curry**

Beyond limits. "Your limits are somewhere up there, waiting for you to reach beyond infinity."

— **Arnold Henry**. A former NCAA Division I basketball player, he is a writer, a motivational speaker, and a skill development basketball trainer who strives to inspire youth through the use of his personal life experience.

Lebron and a tree.

Q. What's the difference between Lebron James and a tree?

A. A tree has more rings.

No dunking for you! The slam dunk is exciting, but did you know that from 1967 to 1976 the NCAA banned it?

Ban dunking? That's crazy! Why?

Kareem Abdu-Jabbar, then known as Lew Alcindor, couldn't be "stopped" from dunking. So, the NCAA felt they had to try and limit this unstoppable dominance, and banned dunking. They allowed it again in 1976.

Kareem Abdul-Jabbar

Don't have to be tall to dunk. Dunking contests don't have to be won by the tallest people, of course. Did you know the 5-foot 7-inch Atlanta Hawks guard, Spud Webb won the 1986 NBA Slam Dunk Contest? Check it out on YouTube (see the link in the references) where Spud Webb shocked the world by beating teammate Dominique Wilkins to win the 1986 NBA Slam Dunk Contest. [7]

Do the job and the rest will take care of itself. "All I know is, as long as I led the Southeastern Conference in scoring, my grades would be fine."

-- **Charles Barkley**

Who is the only NBA player to play in 4 decades? He was known as "Vinsanity", "Air Canada", and "Half Man, Half Amazing! None other than the 360-degree windmill jumping dunk slammer, Vince Carter. Many experts regard him as the GOAT dunk master.

Vince Carter

Basketball, Life Jackets, and Crocs. It might be a good idea to wear a life jacket on the only floating basketball court in the world. On Lake Tonie Sap, the village of Chong Khneas has the only floating basketball courts in the world. Basketball is played where catfish, freshwater dolphins and crocodiles are plentiful.

In Lake Tonle Sap, Cambodia, 1.4 million people live in floating villages in Cambodia with another 4 million living on the banks.

As part of their adjusting to the rainy season, they have a floating pig farm, two floating schools, a floating community market, a Catholic church, and a Buddhist temple that floats on the lake.

During the rainy season, the basketball court sits out in the middle of the lake. It rests on shore when it's not rainy season.

Goals. "It's not about getting out of your comfort zone to reach your goal. It's about widening your comfort zone so far that your goal fits comfortably inside. Once you do that, hitting your goals will be like hitting 3s for Steph Curry."

— **Richie Norton**

Making plays one way or another. "He makes plays you can't coach, and he makes plays that look like he's never been coached."

    -- **Bill Self.** Comment on point guard Tyshawn Taylor

Getting older won't stop me. "I play in the over-40 basketball league. We don't have jump balls. The ref just puts the ball on the floor and whoever can bend over and pick it up gets possession." – Anon.

Missing shots. "I've missed more than 9000 shots in my career. I've lost almost 300 games. Twenty-six times, I've been trusted to take the game winning shot and missed. I've failed over and over and over again in my life. And that is why I succeeded."

    -- **Michael Jordan**

We're not moving. The fans love us. NBA teams relocate from time to time to other cities due to crowd attendance and players' needs. But did you know that out of the 30 NBA teams, the Celtics and Knicks are the only teams to have never moved!?

Street ball. "You ready to play?" Dave asked, bouncing it.

"I don't know," I said. "Are you going to cheat?"

"It's street ball!" He said chucking it to me. "Show me that love."

"So cheesy," I thought. But as I felt it, solid against my hands, I did feel something. I wasn't sure it was love. Maybe what remained of it, though, whatever that might be. "All right," I said. "Let's play."

— **Sarah Dessen**, novelist brief excerpt from "What Happened to Goodbye."

Slam-dunk limitation. "I haven't been able to slam-dunk the basketball for the past five years. Or, for the thirty-eight years before that, either."

-- **Dave Barry**

The first college basketball game. In 1896, the first collegiate game took place between the University of Chicago and the University of Iowa in Iowa City.

Each team only had 5 players and did not use substitutes. The University of Chicago won 15-12.

Being remembered. "If all I'm remembered for is being a good basketball player, then I've done a bad job with the rest of my life."

— **Isiah Thomas**. Twelve-time NBA All-Star was named to the NBA's 50th and 75th anniversary teams, and inducted into the Naismith Memorial Basketball Hall of Fame.

No offense, King James. Many say the only difference between Lebron James and Nikola Jokic is that Lebron can jump higher.

When Jokic heard that he said, "That is offensive…Just kidding! To be compared with of the greatest who's ever played is really cool."

-- **Nikola Jokic**

Why is the hoop called a basket? Basketball was originally played with a soccer ball and peach baskets. The problem was the basketball referees had to get the soccer ball out of the peach basket when a team scored.

So, string baskets were introduced in 1900.

Backboards were introduced sometime later to stop spectators from interfering with the ball and blocking shots.

What do you call it? "Yeah, Ernie, it's called 'Defense', I mean, I wouldn't know anything about it personally, but I've heard about it through the grapevine."

-- **Charles Barkley**

Basketball Rule Question 3. Big Mo is 7 feet tall 220 lbs. and is running frantically to the sideline trying to stop a ball going out of bounds. He realizes he won't be able to make it and takes a big swing at the ball with his fist trying to punch it back in bounds.

Big Mo was just able to punch it back in with his fist. But Mo couldn't stop his momentum and spearheaded into Sam, a spectator in the stands. Sam was holding a beer that was splashed all over as well as knocking Sam out of his seat. What's the ruling, if any?

A. Big Mo must apologize and buy Sam another beer.

B. The referee does nothing. Big Mo kept the ball in bounds and play continued.

C. The referee rules turnover since Big Mo punched the ball.

D. Sam is given a season's pass to the rest of the home games.

Answers begin on p. 97.

C'mon coach! A college basketball coach walked into the locker room before a game, looked over to his star player, and said, "I'm not supposed to let you play since you failed math, but we need you in there. So, what I have to do is ask you a math question, and if you get it right, you can play."

The player agreed, and the coach looked into his eyes intently and asked, "Okay, now concentrate... what is two plus two?"

The player thought for a moment and then he answered, "4?"

"Did you say 4?!?" the coach exclaimed, totally excited that he got it right!

The coach's excitement didn't last long when all the other players on the team began shouting, "Come on coach, give him another chance!"

Virginia basketball players are smart. "I know the Virginia players are smart because you need 1500 SAT to get in. I have to drop breadcrumbs to get our players to and from class."

    -- **George Raveling,** former player and coach.

Winning is overrated. "The only time winning is really important is in surgery and war."

    -- **Al McGuire**

Aboard a basketball court. On the USS Carl Vinson, an aircraft carrier, that was utilized during the Iraq War and also used for the at-sea burial of Osama bin Laden after he was killed in 2011.

That carrier served as a court for the "Carrier Classic" which pitted Michigan State vs. North Carolina.

President Obama attended it to see the game on Veteran's Day. It was the only game ever held on a carrier. There was a scheduled game on another carrier, the USS Yorktown in Charleston Harbor, South Carolina, but that game was canceled due to condensation on the court.

Bill Bradley. A former US Senator, and now 79 years old, was an all-state basketball player in high school and offered 75 college scholarships. He turned them all down to attend Princeton University. He was the NCAA Player of the Year in 1965, when Princeton finished third in the NCAA Tournament.

After graduating in 1965 he attended Oxford on a Rhodes Scholarship where he was a member of Worcester College, delaying a decision for two years on whether or not to play in the National Basketball Association (NBA).

While at Oxford, Bradley played one season of professional basketball in Europe. Later he joined the New York Knicks in the 1967–68 season, after serving six months in the Air Force Reserve and spent his entire ten-year professional basketball career playing for the Knicks, winning NBA titles in 1970 and 1973.

Here is one description of his warm-up. "Bradley is one of the few basketball players who have ever been appreciatively cheered by a disinterested away-from-home crowd while warming up. This curious event occurred last March, just before Princeton eliminated the Virginia Military Institute, the year's Southern Conference champion, from the NCAA championships.

"The game was played in Philadelphia and was the last of a tripleheader. The people there were worn out, because most of them were emotionally committed to either Villanova or Temple-two local teams that had just been involved in enervating battles with Providence and Connecticut, respectively, scrambling for a chance at the rest of the country.

"A group of Princeton players shooting basketballs miscellaneously in preparation for still another game hardly promised to be a high point of the evening, but Bradley, whose routine in the warmup time is a gradual crescendo of activity, is more interesting to watch before a game than most players are in play.

"In Philadelphia that night, what he did was, for him, anything but unusual. As he does before all games, he began by shooting set shots close to the basket, gradually moving back until he was shooting long sets from 20 feet out, and nearly all of them dropped into the net with an almost mechanical rhythm of accuracy.

"Then he began a series of expandingly difficult jump shots, and one jumper after another went cleanly through the basket with so few exceptions that the crowd began to murmur.

"Then he started to perform whirling reverse moves before another cadence of almost steadily accurate jump shots, and the murmur increased.

"Then he began to sweep hook shots into the air. He moved in a semicircle around the court. First with his right hand, then with his left, he tried seven of these long, graceful shots-the most difficult ones in the orthodoxy of basketball-and ambidextrously made them all.

"The game had not even begun, but the presumably unimpressible Philadelphians were applauding like an audience at an opera."

— **John McPhee**, A brief excerpt from, "A Sense of Where You Are: Bill Bradley at Princeton."

Bill Bradley.

Coach's persona. "A team should be an extension of a coach's personality. My team is arrogant and obnoxious."

-- **Al McGuire**

Coordinated for sure. Did you ever see Michael Jordan switch hands in midair? In game 2 of the 1991 NBA finals against the Lakers, MJ was going in for a dunk and in midair switched the ball from his right to left hand to avoid a block by an oncoming player.

Opportunity knocks. "We are in the business of kicking butt, and business is very, very good.

"I remember sitting down with the Rockets and saying, 'Yeah. I'm going to retire.'

"They said, 'Well, we'll give you $9 million.'

"And I said, 'You got a pen on you?'"

    -- **Charles Barkley**

Strange operation. Michael Jordan is wheeled into the hospital for emergency surgery.

He's brought into the operating room and meets his doctors, but he notices something strange. In the corner, there's a stage being set up. An anesthesiologist is repeating jokes to herself and wiping her brow. The MRI techs are handling a soundboard in the back. The head surgeon is tuning a guitar by his bed.

"Hey doc, what's exactly going on here?" MJ asks.

The doctor smiles. "Open Mike Night."

Did you know this about Kobe? Kobe decided not to attend college and declared himself eligible for the NBA draft when he graduated from high school.

The Charlotte Hornets chose him with the 13th pick of the 1996 draft. Then a short time later traded him to the Lakers.

Kobe is the fourth youngest NBA player in history and when he started playing, he was then the second youngest player in NBA history when the 1996–97 season opened. [8]

100%! "We're shooting 100 percent – 60 percent from the field and 40 percent from the free-throw line."

　　-- **Norm Stewart.** Most of his coaching career was with the University of Missouri from 1967 until 1999. He retired with an overall coaching record of 731–375 in 38 seasons.

Talent is God-given.

"Be humble.

Fame is man-given.

Be grateful.

Conceit is self-given.

Be careful."

> **-- John Wooden**

A good thing. "Good thing in this business is that you just have to make one big shot and that's enough to make you forget 9 other shots that you missed."

> — **Guy Zucker**. Former player and agent.

No success the first time? It all depends on the sport. If at first you don't succeed, give up skydiving and try basketball.

Lakers v. Celtics. A Lakers fan, a Celtics fan, and a Bulls fan are climbing a mountain and arguing about who loves his team more.

The Bulls fan insist he's the most loyal. "This is for the Chicago Bulls!" he yells and jumps off the side of the mountain.

Not to be outdone, the Lakers fan is next to profess his love for his team. He yells, "This is for the Los Angeles Lakers!" and pushes the Celtic fan off the mountain.

I look at it this way. "It looks like a stickup at 7-Eleven. Five guys standing there with their hands in the air."

-- **Norm Sloan**, commenting on zone defense.

Teammates. "Ask not what your teammates can do for you. Ask what you can do for them."

-- **Magic Johnson**

Rising star. Perhaps a strong up and coming star. Luka Doncic. In 2015 he joined the academy at Real Madrid at the age of 16 and was the youngest in club history. Then three years later, he led Madrid to the 2018 EuroLeague title, winning the Final Four MVP. He then won back-to-back EuroLeague Rising Star and ACB Best Young Player awards.

In 2018, he played for the Dallas Mavericks and was selected unanimously to the NBA All-Rookie First Team and won

Rookie of the Year for the 2018–19 season. In his next four seasons, he was selected to the NBA All-Star game and named to the All-NBA First Team.

He is the Mavericks' franchise leader in career triple-doubles. [9]

Luka Doncic

Tall wonder. The 7-foot college freshman decided to try out for the basketball team.

"Can you dunk?" asked the coach.

"Watch this," said the freshman, who proceeded to slam dunk the ball with so much force it shattered the backboard.

"Wow!" said the coach. "I'm impressed. Can you run?"

"Of course, I can run," said the freshman. He was off like a rocket and ran the court in just a few seconds.

"Great!" enthused the coach. "But can you pass a basketball?"

The freshman hesitated for a few seconds. "Well, coach," he said, "if I can swallow it, I can probably pass it."

Can't do it alone. "One man can be a crucial ingredient on a team, but one man cannot make a team."

    -- Kareem Abdul-Jabbar

Half-time conversation.

Joe – "My buddy opened a tavern for basketball players."

Moe -- "I heard about that, and it's been catching on. Others are doing too."

Joe – "Competition doesn't bother him since he knew it was a great thing, so he set the bar very high."

Basketball spreads. The U.S. was the first country to play basketball. And the first country to play basketball outside of the U.S. was Canada in the late 1800s. In 1893, basketball spread to France, then England followed in 1894. Shortly thereafter, it spread to Australia, China, and India. Then it was played in Japan in 1900.

Bury me this way. "When my time on earth is gone, and my activities here are passed, I want they bury me upside down, and my critics can kiss my ass!"

‑‑ **Bobbie Knight**. Nicknamed "the General", Bobbie won 902 NCAA Division I men's college basketball games, a record at the time of his retirement, and currently fifth all-time. He's best known as the head coach of the Indiana Hoosiers from 1971 to 2000

A Miami Heat fan. A Miami Heat fan was asked these questions and here are his answers.

Q. What do you call 10 Denver Nuggets fans on the moon?

A. A problem.

Q. What do you call 100 Denver Nuggets fans on the moon?

A. A problem.

Q. What do you call 1000 Denver Nuggets fans on the moon?

A. Still a problem.

Q. What do you call all of the Denver Nuggets fans on the moon?

A. PROBLEM SOLVED!

Secret. "The secret is to have eight great players and four others who will cheer like crazy."

-- **Jerry Tarkanian.** College basketball coach for 31 seasons over five decades at three schools. He spent the majority of his career coaching with the UNLV Runnin' Rebels, leading them four times to the Final Four of the NCAA Division I men's basketball tournament, winning the national championship in 1990.

The popularity grows! In its early years, basketball boosted membership of YMCAs since the YMCAs had courts but there weren't many other places to play.

As basketball became more and more popular, some YMCAs prohibited basketball since their gyms were being dominated and wholly taken up by the sport and no one else was able to enjoy the gym.

So, people began to quit their membership and the YMCA suffered what was turning out to be a big loss in membership.

So, the YMCAs began renting halls so members could use them to play basketball.

Another March Madness fact. Buckeyes v. Bearcats. In 1961, the top-ranked team was Ohio State. They reached the final and played for the Championship against the University of Cincinnati. This was the first time in history that both teams from the same state played in the Championship game. Cincinnati won it against the defending champions Ohio by 70-65.

Basketball rule #3. Streakin' Sammy is racing down the court thinking he's all alone and ready to do a smooth layup when out of nowhere comes Flyin' Freddie and cleanly blocks the layup.

Sammy's outraged! Freddie sticks his thumbs in his ears, sticks his tongue out, and wiggles his fingers at Sammy. The referee blows the whistle. Why did the referee stop play?

Answers begin on p. 97.

Be like Mike. In New York City the creative agency AKQA used the 2015 NBA All-Star Game festivities to give people an opportunity to relive some of Michael's greatest moments.

They created a half-court surrounded by white walls. With the touch of a button, those walls came alive showing famous moments in Mike's career like his game-winner against the Utah Jazz while playing for the Chicago Bulls. They also showed Mike's amazing corner jumper that won the NCAA championship while playing for North Carolina.

AKQA also had a production company called Stardust, which hired 250 actors who dressed the part of fans by what was fashionable in the 80s including big mustaches and mullets. Talk about getting in the spirit!

They shot the ball well early. But, when you're hot you're not always hot…"What comes out of the microwave hot doesn't always stay hot. I know because I eat bagels in the morning."

    -- **Shaquille O'Neal**

Widen your comfort zone. "It's not about getting out of your comfort zone to reach your goal. It's about widening your comfort zone so far that your goal fits comfortably inside. Once you do that, hitting your goals will be like hitting 3s for Steph Curry."

    — **Richie Norton**

Who's crap? Years ago, the Chicago Bulls were practicing for an important match when the coach noticed a pile of poo on the basketball court. A pile of poo on the court?!

"Ok guys, who's crap?" he asked his team.

Michael Jordan replied, "Okay sometimes I'm slow going up and down the court, but I'm good in the air!"

Running. "This year, we plan to run and shoot. Next season we hope to run and score."

－－ **Billy Tubbs.** Coached college basketball for 31 seasons over five decades at three schools. He spent the majority of his career coaching with the UNLV Runnin' Rebels, leading them four times to the Final Four of the NCAA Division I men's basketball tournament, and they won the National Championship in 1990.

Spanish question.

Q. What do you call two Spaniards playing basketball together?

A. Juan on Juan

Why I don't play basketball? "I liked the choreography, but I didn't care for the costumes."

－－ **Tommy Tune**, on why he doesn't play basketball. An actor, dancer, singer, theatre director, producer, and choreographer. he has won ten Tony Awards, the National Medal of Arts, and a star on the Hollywood Walk of Fame.

What to do?

Q. What do you do when you see an elephant with a basketball?

A. Get out of the way.

Growing up. "Any American boy can be a basketball star if he grows up, up, up."

    -- Bill Vaughn

Shoes. "These are my new shoes. They're good shoes. They won't make you rich like me, they won't make you rebound like me, they definitely won't make you handsome like me. They'll only make you have shoes like me. That's it."

    -- Charles Barkley

The trophies. "We are in the trophy generation. Give them a trophy for 23rd place. That makes the parents happy."

-- **Tom Izzo**

Groaner. An engineering student, a geometry major, and a star basketball player are trapped on a desert island.

They're debating how to get off the island or get rescued. The engineering student looks around and sees only a few palm trees and some coconuts.

"We need to cut down the trees and make a raft to sail away on," he says and starts designing.

"We need a basketball to pass the time," the basketball player says and walks over to grab a coconut.

The geometry major's eyes light up and he rushes over to help the basketball player set up a hoop.

"Why are you wasting your time helping him instead of me?" the engineering student sneers as he struggles to tie two logs together with palm fronds.

Instead of answering, the geometry major makes a line in the sand a good distance from the makeshift hoop and hands the basketball player a coconut. The basketball player lines up a shot and sinks it with ease.

With a smile, the geometry student turns to the engineering student.

"Because 3 points always make a plane." Then he flies away.

Basketball is like photography. "If you don't focus, you'll only get negative."

> -- **Dan Frisby**

No answer. "Our offense is like the Pythagorean Theorem. There is no answer."

> -- **Shaquille O'Neal**

Free throw question. Slow Joe is trying to get in the zone before he attempts a crucial free throw. He bounces the ball looking at the basket forever for a long time. The referee stops him. What's with the referee?

A. NBA rules say a player can be penalized for taking more than 10 seconds at the foul line. For example, NBA star Dwight

Howard, who was an eight-time All-Star, eight-time All-NBA Team honoree, five-time All-Defensive Team member, and three-time Defensive Player of the Year .has been known to take his time has been penalized for this seldom enforced rule.

It's been reported he takes longer to settle himself as his free throw percentage isn't the greatest. It happened on Christmas Day, on national television, when veteran NBA official Bob Delaney called him on it. [10]

Missed shots are okay. "I'm not against taking shots, but I am against taking bad shots."

    -- **Hank Iba.** Coach and inducted into the Naismith Memorial Basketball Hall of Fame in 1969.

Free throw thoughts? "The real, many-veiled answer to the question of just what goes through a great player's mind as he stands at the center of hostile crowd-noise and lines up the free-throw that will decide the game might well be -- nothing at all."

    — **Wallace David Foster,** Author

Outside shooters. "We have a great bunch of outside shooters. Unfortunately, all our games are played indoors."

-- **Weldon Drew.** Former coach at New Mexico State University. Mr. Drew came to NMSU after coaching high school basketball for Houston's Kashmere High School (485–135 record in 18 seasons), where he left with a 78-game winning streak after winning two consecutive Texas 4A state championships and the high school national championship.

The second longest suspension in NBA history. You may recall the "Malice at the Palace" where Indiana Pacer, Ron Artest got involved in an on-court brawl, between the Detroit Pistons and Pacers in 2004.

The Pacers were up 97-82 with 45 seconds left in the game and Artest got into a shoving match with a Piston player, Ben Wallace. The benches emptied and Ron found himself somehow on the announcer's table trying to get out of the arguments.

It looked like the arguing would end there but a Piston fan in the stands decided to "stir the pot" and hit Ron in the head with a drink.

Artest went into the stands and punched not only the thrower but other fans as well. Ron was joined by other players trying to break it all up, and again, it briefly looked like it would be over, but two fans who perhaps weren't too bright decided to go on the court and get into a fight with Ron and 6-foot 11-inch Jermaine O'Neal.

Ron wound up with an 86-game suspension and fines.

"Malice at the Palace", 2004

By the way, the longest suspension in NBA history was given to O. J. Mayo who violated NBA drug policies that were in effect at that time and the NBA suspended him for two seasons, or 164 games.

Being watched. "A tough day at the office is even tougher when your office contains spectator seating."

-- **Nik Posa**

Winners & Losers. "Basketball is a game with winners and losers, but if you play this game with your heart, you're always a winner."

— **C.M**. Author.

Habits. "Remember that basketball is a game of habits. If you make the other guy deviate from his habits, you've got him."

-- **Bill Russell**

Straight-up basketball. "Scoring 100 points is a lot, but I maybe could have scored 140 if they had played straight-up basketball."

-- **Wilt Chamberlain.** Even though he played over 1,000 games in his 14-year career, he never fouled out. he averaged 2 fouls a game.

Harlem Globetrotter Question. Meadowlark Lemon was an ordained minister and was known for his confetti in the water bucket trick on the court. He also once played trumpet in both The Miles Davis Quintet and the John Coltrane Quartet. Is all of this true or false?

See answer to Globetrotter question on p.

Meadowlark Lemon

3 pointers weren't part of Shaq's game. He only had one 3-pointer in his entire career. Shaquille O'Neal was a four-time NBA champion and a 15 NBA All-Star but only scored one 3 pointer in his career. He attempted it 22 times but only sunk one. Overall, in his career, he had 11,196 buckets.

On February 16, 1996, Magic Johnson inbounded the ball and got it into play with 2 seconds left in the first quarter.

Shaq took it, dribbled it once to control the long pass, took the shot about 5-feet before the arc tossing it with one hand. The ball banked off the backboard and went in as the buzzer sounded.

Shaquille O'Neal

Big dunker. "Big Dunker Dan" breaks away with 7 seconds left with his team down one point and slam dunks the ball shattering the blackboard. The referee stopped play. What's going on with the referee?

A. It's the no-shatter rule. During any game, if a player dunks so hard he shatters the backboard, the point is not counted, and receives a technical foul. The player's intentions don't matter.

Be confident despite everything else. "I can't jump the highest. I'm obviously not the biggest, not the strongest. To excel at the highest level - or any level, really - you need to believe in yourself, and hands down, one of the biggest contributors to my self-confidence has been private coaching.

"There's a reason that I have confidence out there, and it's about how I prepare for games and series and seasons and whatnot, so we've got to stick with that kind of thought process.

"I always have confidence, whether I miss four in a row or make four in a row, that the next one's going in. To a coach, sometimes that might not make sense.

"I just feel so much more comfortable and confident every game I play."

   -- Stephen Curry

School of life. "I think everyone should go to college and get a degree and then spend six months as a bartender and six months as a cab driver. Then they would really be educated."

   -- Al McGuire

The origin of the fast break. University of Rhode Island coach Frank W. Keaney invented the concept of "fast break" in basketball and used it while he was coaching from 1921 to 1948.

Can't talk. "You can say something to popes, presidents and kings, but you can't talk to officials. In the next war, they ought to give everyone a whistle."

-- **Abe Lemmons.** College basketball coach

More quotes from Abe Lemmons.

- On the challenge of coaching versus other professions. "Finish last in your league and they call you idiot. Finish last in medical school, and they call you doctor."

- Abe said to Howard Cosell. "You may be big in New York, but in Walters, Oklahoma, you're nobody."

- On his substitution patterns. "I never substitute just to substitute. I play with my regulars. The only way a guy gets off the floor is if he dies."

- Abe responding to Digger Phelps talking about the pressures of playing at Notre Dame as an 18 or 19-year-old. "I bet that an 18-year-old Marine with his face down in the sand, under fire at Iwo Jima was thinking to himself, 'Gee, I'm glad I'm not a freshman at Notre Dame.'"

- On his center getting only one rebound in the first half. "That's one more rebound than a dead guy."

- "This players getting taller thing is getting out of hand. What we need to do is sink the baskets into the floor at each end of the court and recruit midgets."

Pick me. Victor Wembanyama was selected first overall by the Spurs in the 2023 NBA draft. As most of you know he's 7 feet 5 inches and is now the tallest active NBA player. Manute Bol (7' 7") still holds the record for being the tallest person ever to play in the NBA.

Born in France, Victor learned basketball since it was a family affair. His mother, Elodie de Fautereau, is a basketball coach and former player. She stands 6'3" His father, Felix stands 6'6" Félix, and is Congolese and was a track and field athlete who did the high jump, long jump and triple jump.

His older sister, Eve, plays basketball professionally, and his younger brother, Oscar, has played basketball and handball at the youth level. His grandfather, Michel de Fautereau, played professional basketball, and his grandmother, Marie Christine, also played. [11]

In his first NBA year, he is expected to receive $55 million and is the highest-paid player in the 2023 NBA draft. [12]

Victor Wembanyama

Air Jordan history fact. Did you know when Air Jordan shoes were first introduced and worn by Mike, they were banned by the NBA?

Commissioner, David Stern outlawed them since they matched the Bulls uniform too well being black and red when most all teams had white shoes.

Mike was fined $5,000 for every game he wore them, but he wasn't concerned about the fines since Nike paid them. By the way, Nike made a ton of a lot more in shoe sales.

Basketball Rule Quiz #4. Billy Backside is dribbling close in the front court and past the free throw line with "Quick Pete" who is closely guarding him. Bill knows Quick Pete is fast and steals a lot, so he turns his back to Pete while still dribbling and looking around to either shoot or pass. Many seconds go by, and Billy turns 180 degrees to the basket and shoots. The referee blows the whistle and stops the play. Why did the referee stop play?

A. Billy didn't use deodorant before the game and is stinking up the court.

B. Billy was dribbling for more than five seconds with his back to a defending play in the forecourt.

C. The referee had to go to the bathroom.

D. Pete couldn't see anything with Billy's back to him.

Answers begin on p. 97.

Golf and Basketball. "Everybody asks if putting is like shooting free throws. It has a very similar kind of mindset. And it's just you, the ball, and the target."

    -- Stephen Curry

His Journey. A poem.

"He dribbles quickly,

up to half court,

A shot from this distance,

would be definitely short.

"He looks around,

impatiently scans.

Up on their feet,

the stadium of fans.

"With seconds remaining,

his team is down by one.

This is game seven,

the loser is done.

"He passes to his shooter,

alone on his right.

Who releases the ball,

and he stares at its flight.

"Time sneaks up and

expires on the clock,

Holding his breath,

he can't even walk.

"Finally, the ball,

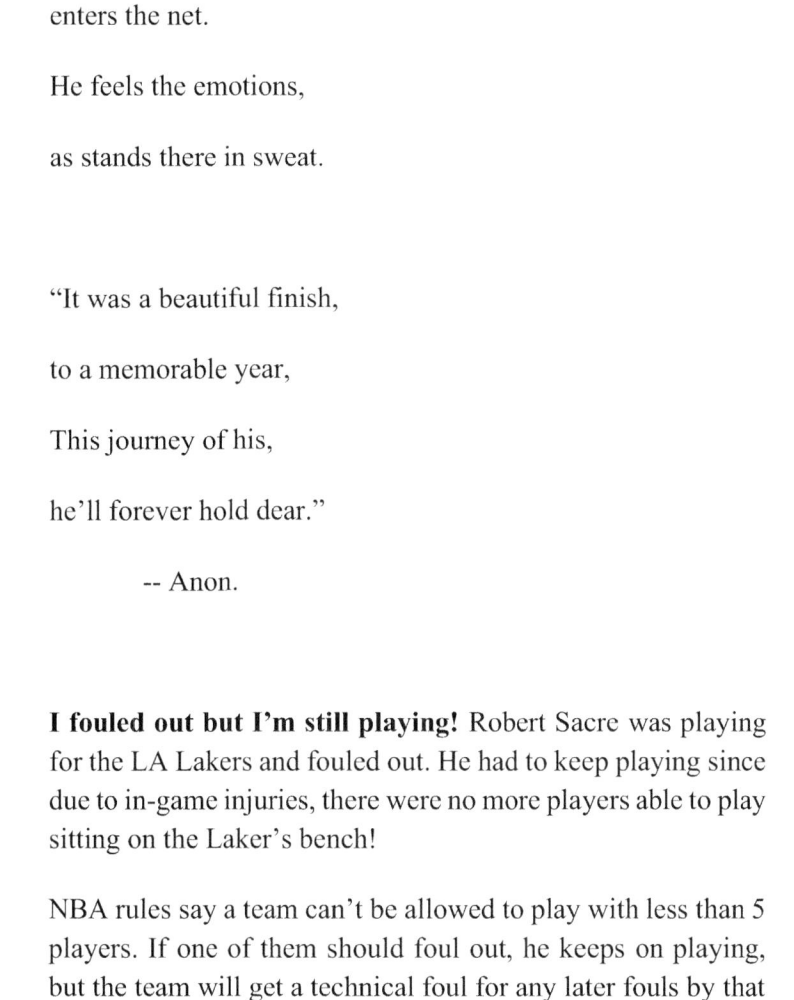

enters the net.

He feels the emotions,

as stands there in sweat.

"It was a beautiful finish,

to a memorable year,

This journey of his,

he'll forever hold dear."

    -- Anon.

I fouled out but I'm still playing! Robert Sacre was playing for the LA Lakers and fouled out. He had to keep playing since due to in-game injuries, there were no more players able to play sitting on the Laker's bench!

NBA rules say a team can't be allowed to play with less than 5 players. If one of them should foul out, he keeps on playing, but the team will get a technical foul for any later fouls by that player.

Not just dog meat. "I knew I was dog meat. Luckily, I'm the high-priced dog meat that everybody wants. I'm the good-quality dog meat. I'm the Alpo of the NBA."

-- **Shaquille O'Neal**

Priorities. "We knew sports was important to us and our family, but there are priorities in life. Obviously, faith is foremost; how we did in school is important. If we didn't handle that business, then there were no privileges."

-- **Stephen Curry**

No gender bias. "My favorite winter sport is women's basketball. Because it's the one time I can yell, "Run faster, play harder, get the move on" at a woman, and no one thinks it's because I'm a sexist pig."

-- Anon.

No thanks. "I really appreciate this award, but I don't want to win it ever again."

-- **Marcus Denmon**, after receiving the Sixth Man Award for the Missouri Tigers.

How's the weather up there? The tallest basketball player ever was a man who was 8.05 ft tall and played for a Libyan team in 1962. His name was Suleiman `Ali Nashnush.

In the NBA, Manute Bol still holds the record for the tallest NBA player ever standing at 7 ft 7 inches. He played for the Washington Bullets and later on the Miami Heat in 1994 and played a total of 624 games and had 1,599 points in his career.

Don't let your height stop you. The shortest NBA player ever was Tyron "Muggsy Bogues" Curtis standing only 5 ft. 3 inches tall. He was known for his aggressive defensive play.

Tyrone Curtis

The first one-handed shot in history. Hank Luisetti who played for Stanford University was the first to use the one-hand shot in the late 1930s.

Prior to that time, outside shots were done using two-handed push shots.

Yeah, yeah, I could do it! "In my prime, I could've handled Michael Jordan. Of course, he would have only been 12 years old."

-- **Jerry Sloan.** NBA player and coach.

Turn around! In 2014, the Rockets played the Thunder, and the Rockets were on top at halftime over the Thunder 73-59. Well, so far so good…

But talk about getting cold, the Rockets only scored 19 points in the entire second half compared to 44 points by the Thunder, and lost the game 104-92.

The crazy thing about this was the Thunder only shot 42.5% in the second half compared to shooting 50% in the first half. Seems the Rockets just got cold and set an NBA record for the biggest point differential between halves.

Good defense. "I want us to play mother-in-law defense: constant nagging and harassment."

    -- Rick Pitino

In the zone. "I've taken countless shots in my life, so you know the ones when you're in rhythm, with a perfect release, and it's on track, that it's going in."

    -- Stephen Curry

Stephen Curry

Losing your cool. A 68-game suspension went to former Golden State Warriors forward Latrell Sprewell. Latrell was enjoying a great career and was chosen for 3 All-Star teams until he couldn't take it anymore from his coach P. J. Carlesimo during a practice session in 1997.

The coach criticized Latrell's passing in a way that didn't agree with Latrell and after more words, he wound up choking the coach but that was broken up and they parted.

That was serious of course. But to make matters worse, Latrell decided, even though the fracas was stopped, to start up again and punched the coach in the face.

Needless to say, Latrell's contract was terminated.

Win them all! "If you make every game a life-and-death proposition, you're going to have problems. For one thing, you'll be dead a lot."

    -- Dean Smith

The GOAT is a matter of opinion. Many think Michael Jordan was the greatest basketball player of all time. He certainly earned more than most with a net worth of over 2 billion.

Others say Bill Russell holds the most wins and championship rings. Wilt Chamberlain has amazing stats. Kareem Abdul-Jabbar played the longest. LeBron James is also amazing. Then there's Stephen Curry and the debates continue.

As the arguments and debates continue, let's pause this for a laugh. What in your opinion was the greatest joke ever told?

Jokes were researched by the FYI International Research whose researchers went over thousands of jokes and narrowed it down to 50 jokes. Then they asked over 36,000 people which was the funniest in their opinion, and this joke came out on top (and you probably heard it before).

A woman gets on a bus with her baby.

The bus driver says: "Ugh, that's the ugliest baby I've ever seen!"

The woman walks to the rear of the bus and sits down, fuming. She says to a man next to her: "The driver just insulted me!"

The man says: "You go up there and tell him off. Go on, I'll hold your monkey for you."

The longest game. The NBA record for the longest game is 78 minutes and happened in 1951. It was a game between the Indianapolis Olympians and Rochester Royals. After 6-overtimes, the Olympians won 75-73.

Well, which way is it? "They say that nobody is perfect. Then they tell you practice makes perfect. I wish they'd make up their minds."

-- **Wilt Chamberlain.** Besides holding the record for scoring 100 points in a single game, Wilt holds the records for most points scored (4,029) and points per game (50.4) in a single season. Both records were set in the 1961–1962 season. He averaged a playing time of 48 minutes per game and averaged a little over 25 rebounds per game.

In the 1959–60 season, he averaged 37.6 points per game and set the rookie record for points scored. Apart from that, the only other NBA player who has more than 3,000 points in a single season, is Michael Jordan in 1986–1987.

Making it. "If you can walk with your head in the clouds and keep your feet on the ground, you can make it in the NBA."

-- **Gary Dornhoefer**

Whatever it takes. "A few years ago, Kobe… fractured the fourth metacarpal bone in his right hand. He missed the first fifteen games of the season; he used the opportunity to learn to shoot jump shots with his left, which he has been known to do in games.

"While it was healing, the ring finger, the one adjacent to the break, spent a lot of time taped to his pinkie. In the end, Kobe discovered, his four fingers were no longer evenly spaced; now they were separated, two and two.

"As a result, his touch on the ball was different, his shooting percentage went down. Studying the film, he noticed that his shots were rotating slightly to the right.

"To correct the flaw, Kobe went to the gym over the summer and made one hundred thousand shots -- that's one hundred thousand made, not taken.

"He doesn't practice taking shots, he explains. He practices making them. If you're clear on the difference between the two ideas, you can start drawing a bead on Kobe Bryant who may well be one of the most misunderstood figures in sports today."

— **William Nack**, a brief excerpt from "The Best American Sports Writing 2008", quoting Scito Hoc Super Omnia by Mike Sager for Esquire Magazine Nov 2007.

It is what it is. "Me shooting 40 percent from the free-throw line is God's way of saying that nobody is perfect."

-- **Shaquille O'Neal**

Highest scoring game ever! In 1983, an amazing game occurred between the Pistons and the Nuggets.

The Pistons won in triple-overtime 186-184.

Isiah Thomas, playing for Detroit, had 47 points, 17 assists, five rebounds and four steals. John Long added 41 points, six rebounds and eight assists.

Kiki Vandeweghe for the Nuggets scored 51 points with nine rebounds and eight assists. Alex English scored 47 points, 12 rebounds, and seven assists.

Detroit shot 54.4 % from the floor 74-for-136. Free throws were 37-for-60.

Denver shot 59.1% from the floor 68-for-115 and 47-57 from the free throw line.

Another amazing game happened in 1992. The Phoenix Suns played host to the Portland Trail Blazers. There were two overtimes and Portland finally won beating Phoenix 153-151 for an amazing combined 304 points.

Character. "Basketball doesn't build character, it reveals it."

-- **James Naismith**

Low percentage? "Right after we signed {George} Gervin, I took him to one of our games and he sat in the stands next to me. After it was over, we walked down to the court. George was wearing a T-shirt, jeans and tennis shoes. He said, 'Why don't they use the 3-point shot more?'

I said, 'Coach [Al] Bianchi doesn't think it's a good percentage shot unless we're behind at the end of the game.'

George said, 'Suppose you could make 15-of-20.'

I said, 'George, that's a really long shot.'

He said, 'But say you could make 15-of-20.'

I said, 'Then Al would probably change his mind.'

The game had been over for a while and the lights were dimmed. It wasn't dark, but it wasn't easy to see the rim, either. George wanted a ball, and someone threw him one. He went behind the 3-point line and started shooting. He took shot after shot and swish after swish.

Then he said, 'That's 18 out of 20.'

I said, 'Hey George, let's go make sure that the ink is dry on your contract.'"

— **Terry Pluto**, quoting Johnny Kerr's brief excerpt from "Loose Balls: The Short, Wild Life of the American Basketball Association."

He's walked the walk. "Push yourself again and again. Don't give an inch until the final buzzer sounds."

    -- Larry Bird

Basketball Rule Quiz Question 5. Joe Jokomo is attempting a free throw after being fouled trying to make a basket. The players take their appropriate positions on the sides. There's a girl in the stands playing music and the song is one of Danny Dancer's favorites. Danny starts moving to the music just as Joe attempts his first free throw and Joe misses.

Do you see any rule violation in this situation?

Answers begin on p. 97.

Most NBA team championships. The record for the most NBA championships won is a tie between the Los Angeles Lakers and Boston Celtics with each having 17.

An interesting thing about the Celtics is they had 7 straight wins from 1960 to 1966.

More about Bill Bradley. "If basketball was going to enable Bradley to make friends, to prove that a banker's son is as good as the next fellow, to prove that he could do without being the greatest-end-ever at Missouri, to prove that he was not chicken, and to live up to his mother's championship standards, and if he was going to have some moments left over to savor his delight in the game, he obviously needed considerable practice.

So, he borrowed keys to the gym and set a schedule for himself that he adhered to for four full years—in the school year, three and a half hours every day after school, nine to five on Saturday, one-thirty to five on Sunday, and, in the summer, about three hours a day."

— **John McPhee**, Brief excerpt "from "A Sense of Where You Are: Bill Bradley at Princeton."

Magic lamp. A Lakers fan and a Celtics fan stumble upon a magic lamp. The Lakers fan gets to it first, picks it up, and gives it a rub.

There's a flash, a puff of smoke, and a genie appears The genie looks at the 2 men and demands to know who it was that rubbed the lamp.

Delighted, the Lakers fan announced that it was him.

"Okay," says the genie, "So you get 3 wishes. But there's a catch."

"What's that then?" asks the Lakers fan.

"Well, whatever you wish for, I'll give the other guy double."

"That's alright with me," says the Lakers fan, and starts the ball rolling by wishing for a million dollars.

"Granted!" says the genie, "But the Celtics fan gets 2 million."

"Fair enough. Now, I'd like a nice new Ferrari,"

"Done. But the Celtics fan gets 2 Ferraris."

"Okay," says the Lakers fan, "For my final wish, I'd like to donate a kidney.

Not figure skating or diving. "This is basketball, not figure skating or diving. You don't get extra points for degree of difficulty."

-- **Bob Hurley.** Amazing High School basketball coach. At the now-closed St. Anthony High School in Jersey City, New Jersey, Hurley amassed 26 state championships in 39 years as a coach. Five of his team have gone undefeated during the season.

Good shots and bad shots. "The only difference between a good shot and a bad shot is if it goes in or not."

-- **Charles Barkley**

Loss for words. Or as one very tired sports announcer says to another, "I don't agree with what you're saying. This is really going to come down to which team scores the most points."

Perfect player. "There is no such thing as a perfect basketball player, and I don't believe there is only one greatest player, either. Everything negative — pressure and challenges — are all an opportunity for me to rise."

-- **Kobe Bryant**

Don't mess with nuns. Four nuns were attending a basketball game. Four beer-drinking drunk men were sitting directly behind them.

Because their habits were partially blocking the view, the men decided to badger the nuns hoping that they'd get annoyed enough to move to another area.

In a very loud voice, the first guy said, "I think I'm going to move to Utah. There are only 100 nuns living there."

Then the second guy spoke up and said, "I want to go to Missouri, there are only 75 nuns living there."

The third guy said, "I want to go to Texas, there are only 50 nuns living there."

The fourth guy said, "I want to go to Maine. There are only 25 nuns living there."

One of the nuns turned around, looked at the men, and in a very sweet and calm voice said, "Why don't you go to hell, there aren't any nuns there!"

Ambidextrous. Did you know that **LeBron James** writes and eats with his left hand but shoots with his right?

Why you might ask? He's gone on record to say he's ambidextrous and when he was young, he tried to imitate Jordan and started shooting with his right and continued doing that.

Simply said. "There are only two options regarding commitment... you're either in or you're out. There's no such thing as life in-between."

    -- **Pat Riley**

College Scholarships. Less than 1 % of high school basketball players play for the NCAA Division 1 Men's Basketball. The odds of a high school basketball player making a Division 1 basketball roster is 105:1, and the odds of a high school basketball player making any college roster is 18:1. [13]

According to the NCSA which is the largest athletic recruiting organization with 35,000 college coach members, these are the things a high school student and parents should be aware of. They point out that each coach has a set of criteria they look for, but these seem to be common and most important.

Compete at the highest level possible playing against the toughest HS teams.

Compete in the summer during live periods. Coaches have more time to view prospects.

Attend elite camps: Besides tournaments, college coaches also evaluate recruits at elite camps – those camps that are the hardest to get into.

Have great academics. Grades matter to coaches, especially Division 1 schools. Good academics show good character.

Send coaches brief excerpts of a video of a High School game where the player shined and showed impressive talent. It's a quick way to get the coaches' attention.

Don't be afraid to talk to coaches. Coaches generally don't have the time to prospect for new talent. Email and call them and send a video.

Apply to the college that would be the best fit. Is there a school nearby where you live? Are you in a region or playing in a tournament known for college recruitment? You might apply to those colleges. [14]

You might be wondering, "What are the best colleges for basketball scholarships?"

Here is a list of the best colleges for basketball scholarships compiled by the NCSA. Learn as much as you can about the particular school you are interested in.

This list shows the best schools and their NCAA divisions. [15]

Top men's basketball colleges: University of North Carolina, UCLA, Stanford University, University of Michigan, University of Florida, University of Virginia, Princeton University, Duke University, University of California, Harvard University.

NCAA Division 1 men's basketball colleges: University of North Carolina, UCLA, Stanford University, University of Michigan, University of Florida, University of Virginia,

Princeton University, Duke University, University of California, Harvard University.

NCAA Division 2 men's basketball colleges: University of California—San Diego, Bentley University, Point Loma Nazarene University, California State Polytechnic University—Pomona, Rollins College, Bellarmine University, California State University—Chico, Western Washington University, Truman State University, Grand Valley State University.

NCAA top Division 3 men's basketball colleges: John Hopkins University, Emory University, Amherst College, University of California—Santa Cruz, California Institute of Technology, Massachusetts Institute of Technology (MIT), Hamilton College, Pomona-Pitzer College, University of Chicago, Trinity University—Texas.

NAIA: Asbury University, University of Michigan—Dearborn, Concordia University—Nebraska, St. Ambrose University, Bethel University—Indiana, Aquinas College—Michigan, College of the Ozarks, Loyola University New Orleans, Taylor University, Indiana Wesleyan University.

Junior Colleges to consider. Florida Southwestern State (FL), Vincennes (IN), Coffeyville (KS), Ranger (TX), John A. Logan (IL), Casper (WY), Odessa (TX), Northwest Florida State (FL), Chipola (FL), South Plains (TX). [16]

The big brother. "Henry had taught Eddie how to play basketball in the playground near the apartment building where they lived--this was in a cement suburb where the towers of Manhattan stood against the horizon like a dream and the welfare check was king.

"Eddie was eight years younger than Henry and much smaller, but he was also much faster. He had a natural feel for the game; once he got on the cracked, hilly cement of the court with the ball in his hands, the moves seemed to sizzle in his nerve endings.

"He was faster, but that was no big deal. The big deal was this -- he was BETTER than Henry. If he hadn't known it from the results of the pick-up games in which they sometimes played, he would have known it from Henry's thunderous looks and the hard punches to the upper arm Henry often dealt out on their way home afterward.

"These punches were supposedly Henry's little jokes--"Two for flinching!" Henry would cry cheerily, and then whap-whap into Eddie's bicep with one knuckle extended--but they didn't FEEL like jokes. They felt like warnings. They felt like Henry's way of saying You better not fake me out and make me look stupid when you drive for the basket; you better remember that I'm Watching Out for You...

"But the most important part of the underneath reason was also the simplest: these things had to be kept secret because Henry was Eddie's big brother, and Eddie adored him."

— **Stephen King**, Brief excerpt from "The Waste Lands."

People talk. So what. "As a professional athlete, a lot is going to be said about you – but I just try to move forward and try to achieve my goals."

-- **LeBron James**

Believe. "Believe that the loose ball that you are chasing has your name written on it."

-- **Mike Krzyzewski,** nicknamed "Coach K", is an American former college basketball coach. He served as the head coach at Duke University from 1980 to 2022, during which he led the Blue Devils to five national titles, 13 Final Fours, 15 ACC tournament championships, and 13 ACC regular season titles.

Sacrifices. "A lot of late nights in the gym, a lot of early mornings, especially when your friends are going out, you're going to the gym, those are the sacrifices that you have to make if you want to be an NBA basketball player."

-- **Jason Kidd**

Practical Ways to get a college scholarship. The first thing is obvious. Practice, practice, practice and play as much as you can. Start early and get on a team at your earliest opportunity.

WikiHow suggests considering joining the Amateur Athletic Union (AAU) team (they have different age group teams) in your area since the AAU promotes amateur sports in the US. While playing on your high school team is vital for getting a scholarship, you can increase your chances by joining a team outside of school as well. Not only will you be playing more basketball, but you'll also be able to develop your game by playing with different players. [17]

Playing for more than one team will show dedication, drive and a keenness for basketball. And AAU tournaments attract college coaches. Google AAU to find one in your area.

Summer camps of course. See the website and check out basketballcampsusa.com for a camp in your area.

The NCAA also has a website of the most elite basketball showcase camps: https://web3.ncaa.org/bbcs/publishedEvents.

Great grades are good since recruiters shy away from bad grades and you should try to improve on your weakest subjects.

You might consider taking your SATs and ACTs as early as you can since the earlier you take these exams, the more opportunities you will have to repeat them. If you don't get the scores, you want the first time, take the exams again. Better scores mean better chances.

NCAA schools have curriculum requirements for scholarships that include 16 core courses in high school, and you might have to earn at least a 2.0 GPA or better in those 16 courses, meet the sliding scale requirement of the SATs and ACTs, and graduate from high school. [18]

Make a list of colleges you want to apply to and hope to get a scholarship. Learn as much as you can about the school.

Talk to career guidance counselors at your high school to get their views on scholarships and schools that interest you.

Speak to the career guidance teacher at your high school to find out which colleges and scholarships are best suited to you.

Create a detailed personal resumé for colleges and coaches giving information about yourself, your grades, any awards, your statistics and playing history, and anything else that might interest them and the school board. Putting your grades first shows you value education.

Have a video made of your ability in game competition and highlights. You might consider keeping the video brief since a coach's time is valuable. Pick your best moments and edit them. Have the video show all parts of your game, such as defending, passing, moving, and scoring.

WikiHow has a lot more advice on things you can do to further your chances of getting that scholarship. See the article in the link in the references of this book. [19]

It is best to always be polite since being polite shows you would be an asset to their college program.

Basketball Rule Quiz Question 6. Peter Point Guard is coming down the court doing low dribbles, speed dribbles, change of pace dribbles, cross-over dribbles, reverse dribbles, and hockey dribbles.

The crowd is going nuts at the show and all eyes are on Peter except Freddie Forward who is trying to get free from Danny Defender. Freddie shoves Danny to the floor and the referee calls a foul.

Peter, wanting to continue his show for the crowd frustratingly throws the ball far down the court to one of the referees, not noticing another referee just 6 feet to his left. The referee to his left blows his whistle. What's the call?

Answers begin on p. 97.

Chuck Norris joke. Michael Jordan to Chuck Norris: "I can spin a ball on my finger for over two hours. Can you?"

Chuck Norris: (laughs) How do you think the earth spins?

Good coaches. "Good coaches tell you where the fish are, great coaches teach you how to find them."

— **Kobe Bryant**, from "The Mamba Mentality: How I Play."

Focus. "I would tell players to relax and never think about what's at stake. Just think about the basketball game. If you start to think about who is going to win the championship, you've lost your focus.

-- **Michael Jordan**

A nice choice that worked well. "I was wrestling all the way to high school, but it kind of came in the same season as basketball, so I had to pick and choose one, and I decided to go all the way with basketball."

-- **Tyrone Curtis "Muggsy" Bogues**, 5' 3" the smallest player ever to make the NBA.

The nature of defense. "Defense is just hard work. There will be nights when your shots won't fall, but you can play good defense every night."

-- **Red Auerbach**

It's only one miss.

> "...it's
>
> just one miss, but
>
> you're gonna have
>
> a whole lotta makes
>
> in this life, 'cause you're just
>
> that good, and it's okay
>
> to be down
>
> and upset
>
> as long as
>
> you're not down
>
> and out."
>
> — **Kwame Alexander**, excerpt from "Rebound."

Work for it. "To achieve positive results, one must work for them, not hope for them.

"Basketball is a full-court game, so every drill must be done full court.

"Passing is your best weapon against man-to-man. Dribble penetration is your best weapon against a zone.

"The single most important aspect of coaching is running effective practices."

    -- Bobby Knight

Being unselfish. "Create unselfishness as the most important team attribute."

    -- Bill Russell

An old one. The Detroit Pistons manager flies to Mogadishu to watch a young Somalian play basketball and is suitably impressed and arranges for him to come over.

Two weeks later Pistons are down 78-54 after three quarters. The coach gives the young Somalian a chance to play, and he goes in.

He's a sensation and shoots three after three – he can't miss! He levels the score at 84-84 with only a few seconds left then miraculously throws one from mid-court right through the net. The fans go wild! The coach, the rest of the team and everyone love him as the media surrounds him!

After the game, he calls his mom. "Hello mom, guess what?" he says, "I played the last quarter and won the game coming from behind! Everybody loves me, the fans, the media, they all love me."

"Wonderful," says his mom. "Let me tell you about my day. Your father got shot in the street and robbed, your sister and I were ambushed and beaten, and your brother has joined a gang of drug dealers and looters, and all while you were having such great time."

The young man is very upset. "What can I say mom, but I'm really sorry."

"Sorry? Sorry?" says his mom, "It's your stinking fault we came to Detroit in the first place!"

Being great. "Great players are willing to give up their own personal achievements for the achievement of the group. It enhances everybody."

> -- **Kareem Abdul-Jabbar**

The longest shot. Harlem Globetrotter Corey "Thunder" Law has several records and holds the record for the longest successful basketball shot at 109 ft 9 in.

He also holds the record for the longest basketball shot blindfolded at 69 ft 6 in and the farthest shot backward at 82 ft 2 in.

Haven't thought of this before. If basketball had never existed, Michael Jordan would've been just a normal guy. Maybe I'm the best player of a sport that doesn't exist and that's why I'm a normal guy.

Fork in the road. "All great athletes essentially come to a fork in the road where they have to change their approach to succeed. It's a sign of intelligence and character.

"My college coach, Jack Hartman, made me play only defense for a full year in practice when I became academically ineligible for my junior year at Southern Illinois.

"Embarrassed, I thought at first about arguing with Coach Hartman over what I felt was a tremendous slight. But instead,

I started lifting weights and working so hard on my defense that my teammates hated to see me match up against them in practice.

"That was the turning point of my life, on and off the court."

— **Walt Frazier**, brief excerpt from "The Game Within the Game." Walt led the New York Knicks to the franchise's only two championships and was inducted into the Naismith Memorial Basketball Hall of Fame in 1987

A billion basketballs. "One billion b-balls dribbling simultaneously throughout the galaxy.

"One trillion b-balls being slam dunked through a hoop throughout the cosmos.

"I can feel every single b-ball that has ever existed at my fingertips, I can feel their collective knowledge channeling through my veins. Every jump shot, every rebound and three-pointer, every layup, dunk, and free throw. I am there."

— **Charles Barkley**

The worst shock. "I still suffer hate and pain in my heart every time I see the word "Duke" on a TV screen, and that rotten thing happened nine years ago when that Swine Christian Laettner hit that impossible last-second shot against Kentucky. I still have a Memory Block about it -- but as I recall it was in the East Regional final that is still known as 'the Best basketball game ever played.'

"Geez, it Was and remains the Worst Shock I've experienced in my Life."

— **Hunter S. Thompson**, a brief excerpt from "Hey Rube: Blood Sport, the Bush Doctrine, and the Downward Spiral of Dumbness: Modern History from the ESPN.com Sports Desk."

Practicing. "Champions play as they practice. Create a consistency of excellence in all your habits."

-- **Mike Krzyzewski**

Fastest mile dribbling. According to Guinness World Records, the fastest mile running record is held by the Moroccan Olympic medalist Hicham El Guerrouj with a time of 3 minutes 43.13 seconds. But what is the fastest time for running a mile while dribbling a basketball?

Guinness World Records says the fastest mile dribbling a basketball is 4 min 28.06 sec. That was done by Max Aronow in West Hartford, Connecticut, on 15 October 2022. Max broke his own record of 4 min 30.38 sec. in 2020. [20]

Banana split with a milkshake. There are many basketball plays but did you ever see the Harlem Globetrotters do the "Banana Split with a milkshake?"

Hammer the Globetrotter's center shouts, "Banana split with a milkshake!" Immediately everyone starts running circles around their usual foe, the Washington Generals, passing the ball over and over again when one of them finally dunks just as the play clock expires.

Harlem Globetrotters v. Washington Generals

Strength. "The strength of the team is each individual member. The strength of each member is the team."

-- **Phil Jackson**

Role challenge. "Sometimes a player's greatest challenge is coming to grips with his role on the team."

    -- **Scottie Pippen**

The best teams have chemistry. "They communicate with each other, and they sacrifice personal glory for the common goal."

    -- **Dave DeBusschere**

Making the best out of a bad situation. Hurricane Katrina hit New Orleans in 2005 with tremendous force leaving vast damage. Did you know that Kelly Oubre Jr. was born in New Orleans? After Hurricane Katrina hit there, his family moved from New Orleans to Texas and Kelly began playing high school basketball at George Bush High School in Richmond. Then in his senior year, he transferred to Findlay prep school near Las Vegas.

During his senior year, he agreed to go to the University of Kansas to help the Jayhawks. Now with the Hornets, coach Steve Clifford said, "Oubre's got size, instincts, feel for the game. But most importantly, he's confident and poised and he's smart." The coach added, "he's got to get bigger, stronger, more experienced, but he has a chance to be a really good player."

Sometimes a terrible storm produces events that lead to great success.

Kelly Oubre, Jr.

Playing the right way. "Play the right way means play unselfishly, respect each other's achievements, play hard, and fulfill your role."

-- **Gregg Popovich**

Rhythm. "Basketball is a beautiful game when the five players on the court play with one heartbeat."

-- Dean Smith

Many, many free throws. In the 2006 NBA Finals between the Miami Heat and the Dallas Mavericks, Miami started the series losing the first two games but came back to win over the Dallas Mavericks and won their first NBA Championship.

However, the series was marred by controversy due to the number of free throws Miami's Dwyane Wade took, especially in the final two games.

During the entire series, Dwayne took a total of 97 free throws, making 75 of them. In the last two games, he had 25 and 21 free throw attempts in games 5 and 6. In the final game, The Mavericks had 25 total free throw attempts in Game 5, while the entire Heat team had 37 total in Game 6.

Mark Cuban, the owner of the Dallas Mavericks, got tired of all the foul calls and free throws and blew up and was fined $250,000 for his shouting profanities at officials and NBA commissioner David Stern.

Mark didn't stop there, he hired a private detective who was a former FBI agent to investigate the entire Championship series.

The agent supposedly found enough evidence to help Mark Cuban win in court, but the billionaire never filed a complaint.

Dwayne Wade

So true. "To many white fans, the Attucks players were like the Harlem Globetrotters, entertainers who had come to play an exhibition.

"But the games meant something quite different to Principal Lane. He viewed each backwoods gym as a showcase for progress and each Attucks player as a goodwill ambassador. A game at a rural schoolhouse was a chance to demonstrate to white fans, some of whom doubtless still had robes and hoods stashed in their closets, that black and white Hoosiers could compete without violence or incident.

"If Hoosiers could observe racial harmony while their sons competed in a packed gym, Lane thought, they would later come to believe in its possibility in schools and neighborhoods."

— **Phillip Hoose**, Brief excerpt from "Attucks! Oscar Robertson and the Basketball Team That Awakened a City."

Lifelong benefits. "Basketball is a lot like life's journey. There are ups and downs, infinite obstacles, and learning discipline and perseverance to succeed. It builds character, teamwork, and creates an ability to move and work together that is essential throughout life."

-- Anon.

My Blood, My Sweat, A Poem.

My blood, my sweat, your tears.

We don't need sticks we've got balls.

Fueled by sweat driven by desire.

Kiss the rim. Nothing but net.

You're not a player if you can't make a pass.

It's not how big you are.

It's how big you play.

-- Anon.

Cool Klay. Many say one special thing about Klay Thompson is he's really not bothered by anyone's opinion. He is his own man with a mind of his own. Say any bad stuff and he disregards the negative. And that he says has made him keep positive even though sports stars face a lot of bad criticism.

Some interesting things about him are that he's got a bulldog named Rocco and he likes to play chess. Reports say he's worth about $38 million and he raised almost $400k for relief charities for California wildfire fires. He's a cool shooter with 1,912 three-pointers in his career.

Klay Thompson

Basketball Rule Question 7. The Aces are playing the Zeros in the final game of the season. Zeros have been in last place all season but in this game, they are only trailing the #1 Aces 56 – 54 with 5 seconds left. Zorro Zero, captain of the Zeros and one of the worst 3-point shooters in the league sets up for a 3-point shot and Joe King of the Aces sees Zorro setting up the shot and immediately asks the referee for a timeout. Prior to Zorro taking the shot, the referee signals for a timeout. Zorro releases the ball after the timeout signal and the shot is good. The game clock signals the end of the game. What's the result?

Answers begin on page 97.

Basketball trivia. In 1891, the very first basketball was not a basketball as we know it today. It all started with men playing basketball with a soccer ball.

Also, in the early days, dribbling was not allowed. They could only throw or pass it from the spot they caught it.

In 1897, the Yale basketball team was the first team to advance the ball by dribbling it. The official rule that allowed dribbling was made 4 years later.

True story. "Kobe was hell-bent on surpassing Jordan as the greatest player in the game. His obsession with Michael was striking. Not only had he mastered many of Jordan's moves, but he affected many of M.J.'s mannerisms as well.

"When we played in Chicago that season, I orchestrated a meeting between the two stars, thinking that Michael might help shift Kobe's attitude towards selfless teamwork.

"After they shook hands, the first words out of Kobe's mouth were 'You know I can kick your ass one on one.'"

— **Phil Jackson**, brief excerpt from "Eleven Rings: The Soul of Success."

Answers to Basketball Rule Questions

Q. 1. Answer is D. In the NBA as well as the International Basketball Federation (FIBA) scoring at your own basket instead of your opponents' is considered illegal especially when it is done intentionally and doesn't count for anything.

This actually happened during an NBA game in November 2009. Almost out of time, Nate Robinson, playing for the Knicks made a strange choice to shoot at his own basket. He missed but if he made the shot before the buzzer, it wouldn't be counted and would result in a turnover to the other team.

Q. 2. A player cannot punch, strike, shoulder-bump, or head-bump to change the trajectory of the ball other than dribbling, holding, and passing. Rule 10, Section IV—Strike the Ball

A player shall not kick the ball or strike it with a fist. Kicking the ball or striking it with any part of the leg is a violation when it is an intentional act. The ball accidentally striking the foot, the leg or the fist is not a violation.

A player may not use any part of his leg to intentionally move or secure the ball.

PENALTY: If the violation is by the offense, the ball is awarded to the opposing team on the sideline nearest the spot of the violation but no nearer to the baseline than the free throw line extended.

If the violation is by the defense while the ball is in play, the offensive team retains possession of the ball on the sideline nearest the spot of the violation but no nearer the baseline than the foul line extended.

If the violation occurs during a throw-in, the opposing team retains possession at the spot of the original throw-in with all privileges, if any.

Q. 3. The referee calls a technical foul since taunting another player is a technical foul. The rule is, "The taunting of opponents isn't permitted, and actions of this nature are to be penalized immediately.

>>Harlem Globetrotter Question. True.<<

Q. 4. Answer is B. One of the most little-known and perhaps little used rule in Basketball is "An offensive player in his frontcourt below the free throw line extended is not allowed to dribble the ball with his back or side to the basket while being actively guarded by an opponent for more the 5 seconds." LeBron James was called for this in a game against the Warriors in May 2023 When he got whistled for a five-second, back-to-the-basket violation while dribbling the ball early in the first quarter.

Q. 5. Joe is given another free throw. Basketball rules say, "During all free throw attempts, no opponent in the game shall disconcert the shooter once the ball is placed at his disposal. The following are acts of disconcertion: (1) Raising his arms when positioned on the lane line on a free throw which will not remain in play, (2) Waving his arms or making a sudden movement when in the visual field of the shooter during any free throw attempt, (3) Talking to the free throw shooter or talking in a loud disruptive manner during any free throw attempt, or (4) Continuing to move during any free throw attempt." Even though Joe missed, he's given another since Danny was moving.

Q. 6. Delay of game! Rule 12.A. Section II says, "A delay-of-game shall be called for…Failing to immediately pass the ball to the nearest official when a personal foul or violation is assessed.

Q. 7. Rule 5, Section VII—Timeout Requests, Section b. 1. says, "If an official, upon receiving a timeout request from the defensive team, inadvertently signals for a timeout during the act of shooting but prior to the release of the ball on a successful field goal or free throw attempt, the point(s) shall be scored." Zeros win!

We hope you enjoyed the book!

If you liked the book, we would sincerely appreciate your taking a few moments to leave a brief review.

Thank you again very much!

Bruce and TeamGolfwell

Teamgolfwell.com

About the authors

Bruce Miller. Lawyer, businessman, world traveler, basketball player and enthusiast, and author of over 50 books, a few being Amazon bestsellers, spends his days writing, studying, and constantly learning of the astounding, unexpected, and amazing events happening in the world today while exploring the brighter side of life. He is a member of Team Golfwell, Authors, and Publishers.

Team Golfwell are bestselling authors and founders of the very popular 340,000+ member Facebook Group "Golf Jokes and Stories." Their books have sold thousands of copies including several #1 bestsellers in Golf Coaching, Sports humor, and other categories.

We Want to Hear from You!

"There usually is a way to do things better and there is opportunity when you find it." - **Thomas Edison**

We love to hear your thoughts and suggestions on anything and please feel free to contact us at Bruce@TeamGolfwell.com

Other Books by Bruce Miller [21] and Team Golfwell [22]

For the Golfer Who Has Everything: A Funny Golf Book.

For a Great Fisherman Who Has Everything: A Funny Book for Fishermen.

For a Tennis Player Who Has Everything: A Funny Tennis Book.

For the Baseball Fan Who Has Everything: A Funny Baseball Book.

For a Fly Fisherman Who Has Everything: A Funny Fly-Fishing Book.

Rules of Golf, A Handy Fast Guide to Golf Rules.

Just Jokes, Adult Golf Humor.

The Funniest Quotations to Brighten Every Day: Brilliant, Inspiring, and Hilarious Thoughts from Great Minds.

Brilliant Screen-Free Stuff to Do with Kids: A Handy Reference for Parents & Grandparents!

And many more…

Index

What you need *1*

Being tall *1*

Makes you wonder *3*

Nervous? *3*

Don't have to like it all the time *4*

March Madness little known fact *5*

Kids are great, but *5*

Basketball Rule Question 1 .... *6*

No limits. *6*

Mistakes *8*

Most points scored by halftime *8*

Anything is possible *9*

More than serious *9*

Individual record for most points *9*

Must pay attention *10*

Hard to get tickets *10*

Selfish and Unselfish *11*

- *Critics in the seats sayings* *11*
- *What a win is like.* *12*
- *Coming alive* *12*
- *Humble beginnings* *12*
- *Just ask me* *14*
- *Making sure you win* *14*
- *You don't need your five best players.* *14*
- *Longest win streak* *15*
- *Not a high scorer?* *15*
- *Don't have to be perfect.* *16*
- *Don't intentionally foul this guy.* *16*
- *Over 50-point games.* *16*
- *It ain't easy.* *17*
- *Beyond limits.* *17*
- *Lebron and a tree.* *17*
- *No dunking for you!* *17*
- *Don't have to be tall to dunk* *18*
- *Do the job and the rest will take care of itself* *19*

For a Basketball Fan Who Has Everything: A Funny Basketball Book

Who is the only NBA player to play in 4 decades? 19

Basketball, Life Jackets, and Crocs. 20

Goals 20

Making plays one way or another 21

Getting older won't stop me 21

Missing shots 21

We're not moving. The fans love us 21

Street ball 22

Slam-dunk limitation 22

The first college basketball game 23

Being remembered 23

No offense, King James 23

Why is the hoop called a basket? 24

What do you call it? 24

Basketball Rule Question 3 24

C'mon coach! 25

Virginia basketball players are smart 26

Winning is overrated 26

For a Basketball Fan Who Has Everything: A Funny Basketball Book

Aboard a basketball court... *26*

Bill Bradley... *27*

Coach's persona. *29*

Coordinated for sure.. *30*

Opportunity knocks *30*

Strange operation *30*

Did you know this about Kobe? *31*

100%!... *31*

Talent is God-given.. *32*

A good thing... *32*

No success the first time?.. *32*

Lakers v. Celtics... *32*

I look at it this way... *33*

Teammates *33*

Rising star... *33*

Tall wonder... *34*

Can't do it alone *35*

Half-time conversation. *35*

Basketball spreads. 35

Bury me this way. 36

A Miami Heat fan. 36

Secret. 37

The popularity grows! 37

Basketball rule #3 38

Be like Mike 38

They shot the ball well early. 39

Widen your comfort zone 39

Who's crap? 39

Running. 40

Why I don't play basketball? 40

What to do? 41

Growing up 41

Shoes. 41

The trophies 42

Groaner. 42

Basketball is like photography 43

No answer *43*

Free throw question *43*

Missed shots are okay. *44*

Free throw thoughts? *44*

Outside shooters. *44*

The second longest suspension in NBA history *45*

Being watched *46*

Winners & Losers. *47*

Habits *47*

Straight-up basketball *47*

Harlem Globetrotter Question. *47*

3 pointers weren't part of Shaq's game *48*

Big dunker *49*

School of life *50*

The origin of the fast break *51*

Can't talk *51*

Pick me *52*

Air Jordan history fact *53*

For a Basketball Fan Who Has Everything: A Funny Basketball Book

Basketball Rule Quiz #4 .... *54*

Golf and Basketball *55*

His Journey. *55*

I fouled out but I'm still playing! *57*

Not just dog meat. *58*

Priorities *58*

No gender bias *58*

No thanks *58*

How's the weather up there? *59*

Don't let your height stop you. *59*

The first one-handed shot in history *60*

Yeah, yeah, I could do it! *60*

Turn around! *60*

Good defense. *61*

In the zone *61*

Losing your cool. *62*

Win them all! *62*

The GOAT is a matter of opinion. *62*

The longest game *63*

Well, which way is it? *64*

Making it *64*

Whatever it takes *64*

It is what it is *65*

Highest scoring game ever! *66*

Character. *66*

Low percentage? *67*

He's walked the walk. *68*

Basketball Rule Quiz Question 5 .... *68*

Most NBA team championships *68*

More about Bill Bradley *68*

Magic lamp *69*

Not figure skating or diving *70*

Good shots and bad shots. *71*

Loss for words *71*

Perfect player *71*

Don't mess with nuns *71*

Ambidextrous *72*

Simply said *73*

College Scholarships *73*

The big brother *76*

People talk. So what *77*

Believe *77*

Sacrifices *77*

Practical Ways to get a college scholarship *78*

Basketball Rule Quiz Question 6 .... *80*

Chuck Norris joke *80*

Good coaches *81*

Focus *81*

A nice choice that worked well *81*

The nature of defense *81*

It's only one miss *82*

Work for it *82*

Being unselfish *83*

Being great *84*

The longest shot. *84*

Haven't thought of this before *85*

Fork in the road *85*

A billion basketballs *86*

The worst shock *86*

Practicing *87*

Fastest mile dribbling *87*

Banana split with a milkshake *88*

Strength *88*

Role challenge *89*

The best teams have chemistry *89*

Making the best out of a bad situation. *89*

Playing the right way *90*

Rhythm *91*

Many, many free throws *91*

So true *92*

Lifelong benefits *93*

My Blood, My Sweat, A Poem *93*

Cool Klay *94*

Basketball Rule Question 7 .... *95*

Basketball trivia *95*

True story *95*

Answers to Basketball Rule Questions *97*

Bruce Miller *101*

Team Golfwell *101*

References

[1] James Naismith, Wikipedia https://en.wikipedia.org/wiki/James_Naismith
[2] Bubba Wells, Wikipedia, https://en.wikipedia.org/wiki/Bubba_Wells.
[3] The Sporting News, https://www.sportingnews.com/us/nba/news/most-points-half-nba-history-full-list-team/ej2afmyl5ghqxc0fn7lqpxwn
[4] Nikola Jokic, Wikipedia,
[5] Ibid.
[6] Longest win streak in the NBA, Wikipedia, https://en.wikipedia.org/wiki/List_of_National_Basketball_Association_longest_winning_streaks
[7] 5-foot-7 Spud Webb wins 1986 NBA Slam Dunk Contest, YouTube, https://www.youtube.com/watch?v=r1YRJvFvlgg
[8] List of oldest and youngest NBA players, Wikipedia, https://en.wikipedia.org/wiki/List_of_oldest_and_youngest_National_Basketball_Association_players
[9] Luka Doncic, Wikipedia, https://en.wikipedia.org/wiki/Luka_Don%C4%8Di%C4%87
[10] Howard gets rare slow free throw foul called, NBC Sports, https://www.nbcsports.com/nba/news/dwight-howard-gets-rare-slow-free-throw-foul-followed-by-technical
[11] Victor Wembanyama, Wikipedia, https://en.wikipedia.org/wiki/Victor_Wembanyama
[12] Here's how much Victor Wembanyama and other 2023 NBA draft picks will earn on their rookie contracts, morningstar.com, "https://www.morningstar.com/news/marketwatch/20230623477/heres-how-much-victor-wembanyama-and-other-2023-nba-draft-picks-will-earn-on-their-rookie-contracts
[13] A Guide to College Basketball Scholarships for High School Students, NCSA College Recruiting, https://www.ncsasports.org/mens-basketball/scholarships

[14] Ibid.
[15] Ibid.
[16] Ibid.
[17] How to get a basketball scholarship, WikiHow, https://www.wikihow.life/Get-a-Basketball-Scholarship
[18] Ibid.
[19] Ibid. at > https://www.wikihow.life/Get-a-Basketball-Scholarship
[20] Fastest Mile dribbling a basketball, Guinness World Records, https://www.guinnessworldrecords.com/world-records/98437-fastest-mile-dribbling-a-basketball
[21] https://www.amazon.com/Bruce-Miller/e/B096C9SN2R?
[22] https://www.amazon.com/Team-Golfwell/e/B01CFW4EQG?